Roger

Ball of Whacks™

A CREATIVITY WORKSHOP IN A BALL

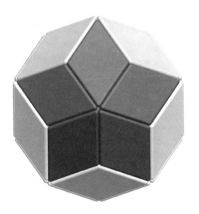

Creative Whack
Stamford, Connecticut   USA

Creative Whack
179 Ludlow
Stamford, CT 06902
United States of America
www.creativewhack.com

Library of Congress Catalog-In-Publication Data
von Oech, Roger V.
    Guidebook to Roger von Oech's Ball of Whacks
    p. 96
    ISBN-10: 0-911121-01-3
    ISBN-13: 978-0-911121-01-8
    1. Creative Thinking. 2. Success. I. Title.

Printed in China.
Written and Designed by Roger von Oech.
Illustrations by George Willett. CAD Renderings by
Jason Hilbourne. Diagrams by Roger von Oech.

To Wendy

By Roger von Oech

A Whack on the Side of the Head
How You Can Be More Creative

A Kick in the Seat of the Pants
Using Your Explorer, Artist, Judge
& Warrior to be More Creative

**Expect the Unexpected
or You Won't Find It**
A Creativity Tool Based on
the Ancient Wisdom of Heraclitus

Creative Whack Pack
64 Creativity Strategies to Provoke
and Inspire Your Thinking

Innovative Whack Pack
60 Heraclitus-Inspired Strategies
to Inspire and Provoke Your Creativity

Ball of Whacks
A Creativity Workshop in a Ball

Acknowledgements

I'd like to thank the following people for their ideas and support in this project: Jason Hilbourne, Dan Corbo, Stuart Kaplan, Steve Holmes, Peter Craig, Celia Ho, Joe Chan, Elias Elftheriades, Dave Gildea, Scott Kim, Peter Macdonald, Brendan Boyle, Bill Seidel, Roger Moirano, Athena von Oech, Alex von Oech, Bob Krolick, Andy Maisel, Barry Katz, Nelson Foo, Mark Corbo, Aaron Hayes, Mark Gordon, Doug Modlin, Elizabeth Kerkstra, Kris Hudgens, Todd Ayers, Jan Hunter, Steve Barretto, Wiley Caldwell, Frank Rodriques, Bill La Fever, George Willett, and Wendy von Oech.

*"Those who approach life
like a child playing a game,
moving and pushing pieces,
possess the power of kings."*

— Heraclitus of Ephesus
Ancient Greek Philosopher,
flourished circa 500 BC

*"It's simple. You just take something,
and then you do something to it.
Then you do something else to it.
And then something else. Keep this up
and pretty soon you've got something."*

— Jaspers Johns
Twentieth century American Artist,
answering the question of what's
involved in the creative process

Contents

"Whole Ball of Wax?"

People often ask me,

"How do you get yourself into a creative mood?"

One of my favorite techniques is to take an object about the size of a ball and then play with it. I'll flip it back and forth from hand to hand. I'll toss it in the air. I'll try grasping it in various ways, or let it roll from finger to finger. Sometimes I just hold it, feel its surface, and let it soothe me. Doing this stimulates a different part of my brain, and gets me into a creative frame of mind.

Indeed, some recent studies have shown that activating your basic motor functions can improve mental performance. I read about a particular one that had two similar groups of people take a mental acuity test. Prior to the test, members of the control group sat quietly in a room for twenty minutes. Members of the target group, however, spent the same time in another room cutting skins off apples with sharp knives. Then both groups took the test. The motor skill-activated group – the apple-parers – performed better. One reason is that a considerable portion of the human brain is dedicated to hand-related functions. So, there's something about getting people's hands and eyes working together that gets their neurons firing!★ For me, the same thing happens when I handle the Ball of Whacks.

For many people, this product's name initially brings to mind its sound-alike cousin, the colloquial expression "whole ball of wax" which is usually understood to mean "everything." The Ball of Whacks doesn't claim to be everything, but it does aspire to be a fun imagination tool you can use to stimulate your creativity. I hope you have fun with it.

If you want to get your hands on the ball right now, go to Part 1 beginning on page 11, and you'll get some ideas for playing with it. If you'd like to use the Ball of Whacks in a creativity workshop, then go to Part 2 on page 39. And, if you'd like to find out more about the Ball's history, geometry, and "golden" nature, go to Part 3 on page 75.

Enjoy playing with your Ball of Whacks!

★ For more on the hand-brain relationship, see page 88.

Part 1:
Play With It

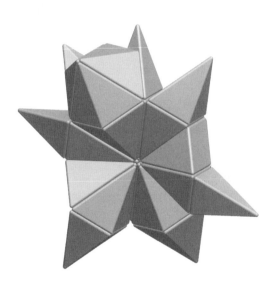

Play With It

A good way to get to acquainted with the Ball of Whacks is to pick it up, take it apart, and start playing with its pieces. That's right! The power and magic of the Ball of Whacks arise from playing with it.

Indeed, I believe that a playful attitude is fundamental to creative thinking. Think about it: you probably generate most of your new ideas when you're just playing around in your mental playground. That's because your assumptions are loosened and you have little concern with the rules, practicality, or being wrong.

You can play with the Ball of Whacks in a variety of different ways:

• Sometimes you'll be a **designer** carefully crafting the Whack pieces together to discover and create new shapes.

• Sometimes your play can be a **meditative activity** in which your engagement with the pieces frees your mind from other concerns.

• There are times when your play is simply a nervous release in which you treat the Whack pieces as so much **"hand candy."**

• And finally, you may wish to engage the Ball in a **creativity workshop** (more on this on page 39).

I encourage to try some of the exercises on the following pages. Not only are they fun, they should also help get your creative juices flowing. And just in case you get frustrated, just remember the Ball's playful motto:

**"The Ball of Whacks:
You Can Handle It!"**

Hold the Ball of Whacks. Pick up the Ball and turn it over in your hands. Notice the different patterns its facets make as you rotate it.

Toss the Ball in the air and catch it. Feels pretty good, right? Try squeezing the Ball without letting the pieces come apart. What things can you stick to the Ball? What places in your room or office you can put the Ball of Whacks? Where would it be most useful? Conspicuous? Surprising?

Say "Hello" to the Whack Piece. Pick up one of the Whack pieces and take a closer look at it. What surfaces can you stick it to? What do you notice about its shape? What other shapes does the Whack piece remind you of? The Great Pyramid of Giza? Dragon teeth? Studs in brass knuckles? A sailing ship? Part of a *sempervivum* succulent plant?

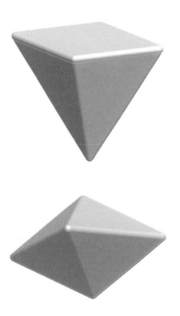

Stars Galore! As you play with the Ball, you'll discover that the number 5 (and also multiples of 5 such as 10, 15, 20, 25, and 30) plays an important role in the types of designs you can craft with its pieces. One beautiful example is the star: it's one of the hallmark shapes you can make with the Ball of Whacks. How many types of stars can you create?

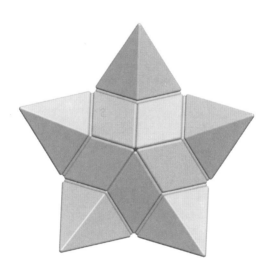

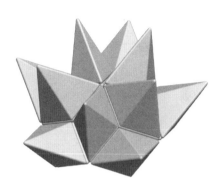

Still More Stars,
Each Made from 15 Whacks

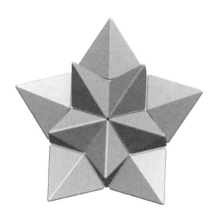

Make A Cube out of "Bow Ties." Take five Whack pieces and make them into the shape displayed below (shown from two perspectives). Let's call this shape a **"bow tie."** Now do this five more times so that you have six different bow ties.

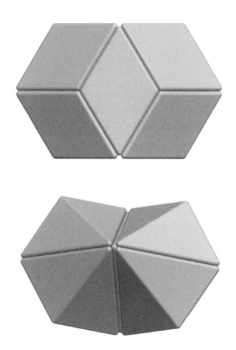

Next, treat each bow tie as one of six sides of a cube and put them all together. Tip: make sure the pointy back side of each bow tie is facing the center of the cube.

Huzzah! You've reassembled the pieces of the Ball of Whacks back into a whole. Notice that when you look at the Ball from this perspective, it does in fact look like a cube.

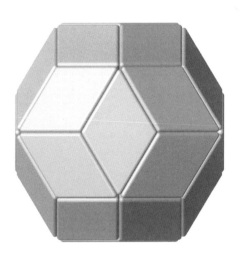

Mosaic-Making. Some versions of the Ball of Whacks come in three different colors of 10 whack pieces each. A fun way to play with this configuration is to keep the pieces in the fully-assembled Ball form, and to focus on making patterns by moving around the individual colors on the Ball's surface. Here are several designs: the "Star" and "Bow Tie" mosaics.

Star Mosaic

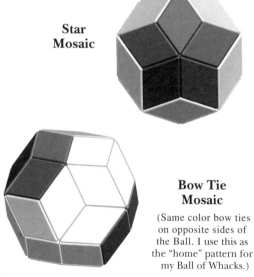

Bow Tie Mosaic

(Same color bow ties on opposite sides of the Ball. I use this as the "home" pattern for my Ball of Whacks.)

The "Grand Mosaic Challenge." Put the whole Ball together in such a way that no edge of one color touches the edge of another similarly colored piece. (Same color point-to-point contact is okay.) This exercise is moderately challenging.★

★Hint: Here's one approach to solving this problem. There are twenty different places on the Ball where three and only three whack pieces converge on a single point (a "3-grouping"). Look at the Ball and see if you can identify all twenty. You might start with one "3-grouping" and make sure that each Whack piece in it is a different color. From there, build your way to the adjacent "3-groupings."

The Wreath of Whacks. Try making a circle by inverting every other Whack piece. This will take some patience on your part, but I think that you'll find this to be a worthwhile construction.

Hand Candy Spinner. Put two pieces back-to-back. Next, put them between your index and middle fingers, and spin them with your other hand. How long can you keep them going? I find this to be quite soothing. It also helps you focus on the simple beauty of the individual Whack piece.

Leave It There. Try making a design where you start with only one piece, and then add just one more piece. Once that second piece has been put in place, you can't change its position. Now add another piece. Same rule applies — you can't change its position once you have placed it. Keep doing this until all thirty pieces have been placed. Try to be aware of your own thinking as you go through this process. How do you feel? Constrained? Freed?

Eyes Closed. Close your eyes and make a shape using some or all of the pieces. Imagine what the shape looks like, and then open your eyes. How close were you?

Ring Challenge. Make a ring of pieces with a hole in it, using as few pieces as possible. You must join pieces so one complete face matches a complete face of another piece. Can you do it with 16 pieces? Can it be done with fewer?

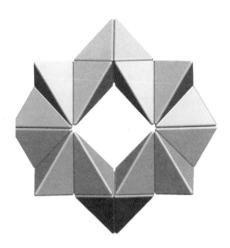

Fun Shapes. What other geometrical shapes can you make?

What animal shapes?

What floral shapes?

What's the longest chain of pieces you can put together?

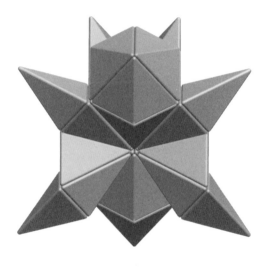

Flying Squirrel

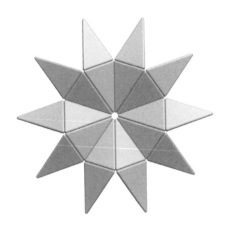

Sunburst and Snow Flake

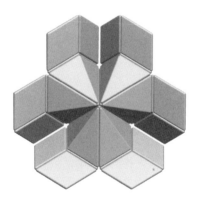

Scorpion and Fertility Icon

House Cat

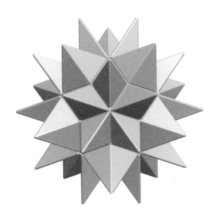

Fully Appointed Ball (Two Views)

"Zen Whack Garden." Perhaps you're familiar with the "Zen Rock Garden." A typical one is a simple rectangular area comprised of several groups of rocks (and perhaps a few plants) which are surrounded by raked-lined sand (or fine gravel). The garden works on two levels: a meditative one and an imaginative one. First, it provides the visitor with a place to quiet his mind and get away from the distractions of the everyday world. And, second, the garden can be a source of mental stimulation: the visitor is invited to look at the garden's simple shapes and objects and use his imagination. Do the rocks look like islands rising from the sea? Puffs of smoke? Clouds? What else?

You can use your Ball of Whacks to create a variation of the Zen Rock Garden. It's the Zen "Whack" Garden. There are three simple steps. **First:** take a metal sheet or metallic surface and place it in front of you. **Second:** place some of the Whack pieces on it. **Third:** relax, play with the pieces, and create some interesting designs. This is one of my favorite ways to use the Whack pieces. It's not only a great meditative activity, it also stimulates your imagination. If you create a design you particularly like, leave it out to inspire you (and others)!

From Sphere to Square. Take all the pieces and spread them out on a metal sheet or a metallic surface. Make a "square" shape like the one below. I think it's neat how each Whack piece can be both "part-Ball" and "part-square."

What other flat shapes can you design on a metal surface? I think you'll find that a lot of different designs will just "come" to you. You might also try making some shapes where all of the pieces do not touch one another.

Spread A Rhombus. Make a multipiece rhombus by spreading the pieces out on a metallic surface. The rhombus is a vital shape in the Ball of Whacks: the base of each Whack piece is a rhombus. Try making a rhombus with 4, 9, and 16 pieces as well. For more information on the rhombus, go to page 76, and also to the section on the "Golden Ratio" on page 82.

Opposite Feelings. Divide the pieces into two sets of 15 Whacks each. Arrange the pieces in one set so that it evokes a feeling, such as "anger" or "serenity." Arrange the pieces in the other set to evoke the opposite feeling. (You may or may not wish to use a metal surface.)

To help you tune into how these shapes can evoke feelings, imagine that the Whack pieces are giant stones arranged in a public park, pieces of furniture in your living room, a setting of stones in a piece of jewelry, or a group of dancers on a stage.

Here are some opposite feelings to try:

- Love — Hate
- Happy — Sad
- Tense — Relaxed
- Calm — Upset
- Easy — Difficult
- Orderly — Chaotic
- Direct — Indirect
- Soft — Hard

You might also try this exercise with another person, with each person taking on one of the opposite feelings.

Changing Shape Story. This game works best with two or more people (but you can also play it by yourself).

1. Make a shape using some or all of the pieces. The shape represents the main character of your story. Say, "Once upon a time there was a . . . ," and describe the character (for example, Fred the dentist, Sylvia the aspiring actress). Then say, "And every day . . . ," and describe something the character did every day (daydreamed about traveling, gave obedience lessons to her dog).

2. Pass the shape to the next person, who changes the shape a little or a lot. This person then says, "But then . . . ," and describes what happens next (fell deeply in love with his neighbor, started a company with her best friend).

3. Keep passing the shape to the next person, who changes the shape and tells the story of what happened next.

4. The last person makes a shape and tells the ending of the story by saying, "Finally, . . . ," and describes what finally happened.

Bridge Challenge. Place two metal surfaces about a foot apart (about 30 centimeters).

Now, use the Whack pieces to build a structure that extends from one of the metal surfaces to the other without touching anything in between.

Cantilever Challenge. Put a metal surface at the edge of a table.

Use the Whack pieces to build a structure that touches only the metal surface, and extend it piece by piece as far as possible out from the edge of the table.

How far can you go?

Speed Challenge. Separate all of the Whack pieces and put them on a flat surface. Now, see how fast you can assemble them into a whole ball.

Summary

Over the years, I've asked many people the following question:

"When do you get your ideas?"

The answers I've received can be grouped into two categories. The first is **necessity,** and it is represented by replies such as: "When I'm faced with a problem"; "when things break down, and I have to fix them"; "when there's a need to be filled"; and, "when the deadline is near — that's the ultimate inspiration." These responses bear out the old adage that "necessity is the **mother** of invention."

But interestingly enough, an equal if not greater number of people get their ideas in the opposite situation, and they respond along these lines: "When I'm just playing around"; "when I'm doing something else"; and, "when I'm not taking myself too seriously." From this I conclude that necessity may be the mother of invention, but **play** is certainly the **father**.

My advice? If you have a problem — or need to take a break — pick up your Ball of Whacks and play with it. It will put you in a frame of mind conducive to generating new ideas.

Here are some things you might try:

- ★ Take it to meetings with you.
- ★ Use it when you're by yourself.
- ★ Use it to relax.
- ★ Throw it in the air.
- ★ Take it apart and rearrange the pieces.
- ★ Make new combinations.
- ★ Experiment: create some wild designs.
- ★ Use it on flat metal surfaces.
- ★ Display the pieces on a whiteboard.
- ★ Combine the pieces with other things such as playing cards, string, paper clips, and other metal and magnetic objects.
- ★ Think of it as a metaphor for your problems.
- ★ And, if you wish, reassemble the pieces back into the original ball.

You'll have a hard time putting it down!

Part 2:
Creativity Workshop

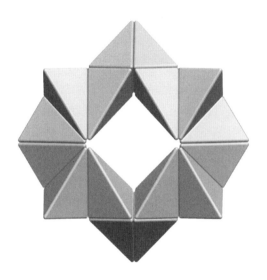

Creativity Workshop

The Ball of Whacks is a kick to play with. It's also a valuable aid in helping you explore your own creative process. But it comes into its full glory when you employ it as an insight-generating tool.

To help you do just that, here are fifteen creativity exercises adapted from my **Creative Whack Pack**. These exercises (on the following pages) are fun and informative, and their lessons can be applied to issues currently before you. Only three simple steps are involved.

One: Think of a problem you're trying to solve, or an issue into which you'd like more insight. Ask yourself, "What aren't I seeing? What should I do next? What's a different approach?"

Two: Pick up the Ball of Whacks. Think of it as a metaphor for your issue. Grasp it. Toss it back and forth. Use it to relax your mind. Think of its pieces as components of your problem.

Three: Now do an exercise and follow the instructions. Take your time. Now, apply the questions at the end of the exercise to your issue.

You might start with exercise #1 and work your way through one by one. Or, if you wish, select an exercise at random. One method for doing this is to go to the page of random numbers on the next page. Then close your eyes and put your finger or pen down on one of the numbers. The number you pick corresponds to the exercise you should do next. For example, if the number you select is 7, your exercise is "See the Obvious" located on page 56.

Why random selection? Since we tend to use the same-problem solving approaches repeatedly, we usually come up with the same answers. A random approach can force us to look at our problems in a way we wouldn't have otherwise, and this can do wonders to stimulate our thinking.

Most exercises will trigger an immediate response. Sometimes, however, you'll encounter one and think, "This doesn't have anything to do with my problem," and be tempted to move on. Don't do it! Often the exercises that initially seem the least relevant become the most important because they point to something you've been completely overlooking.

Good luck and have fun!

01 06 09 10 13 02 03 04 14 09 10 04 02 03 01 12 14 15
04 05 15 02 10 11 12 13 14 01 02 05 06 09 10 13 14 03
04 07 08 11 02 01 12 15 04 06 07 08 09 10 01 02 03 15
05 01 05 15 07 10 01 15 03 10 05 06 05 14 01 05 15 03
06 10 01 02 03 01 10 05 06 05 14 01 05 10 03 04 07 04
11 12 03 10 11 12 13 15 02 03 10 08 06 07 08 11 12 13
14 01 02 05 06 06 10 13 14 03 04 07 08 11 08 15 01 01
02 03 07 11 12 13 14 15 06 06 07 08 09 10 01 02 03 04
05 15 09 10 02 12 13 14 01 02 05 06 09 10 13 14 03 04
07 08 11 09 15 10 11 12 12 14 15 11 06 09 10 13 02 03
04 11 09 10 01 02 03 01 02 14 10 04 05 15 12 10 11 12
13 14 13 02 05 06 09 10 13 14 03 04 07 08 11 13 01 12
15 14 06 07 08 09 10 01 10 03 04 05 15 15 10 05 14 01
01 15 06 10 15 04 07 08 11 02 03 10 11 12 13 15 02 03
10 01 12 13 14 01 02 05 06 09 10 13 14 03 03 07 08 11
12 15 02 01 02 03 10 11 12 13 14 15 03 06 07 08 09 10
01 02 03 04 04 15 02 10 11 12 13 14 01 02 05 15 09 10
13 14 04 07 08 11 12 15 08 11 12 13 14 15 04 06 09 10
13 02 03 04 14 09 06 01 02 03 01 02 14 15 04 05 15 05
10 11 12 13 14 01 02 05 06 09 10 13 14 03 04 07 08 11
01 06 09 10 13 02 03 04 14 09 10 07 02 03 01 10 14 15
04 05 15 02 10 11 12 13 14 01 02 05 06 09 10 13 14 03
04 07 08 11 09 01 12 15 04 06 07 08 09 10 01 02 03 08
05 01 08 15 07 10 01 15 14 10 05 06 05 14 01 05 15 03
06 10 01 02 03 01 10 05 06 05 14 01 11 10 03 04 07 08
11 12 03 10 11 12 13 15 02 03 10 08 06 07 08 11 12 13
14 01 02 05 06 11 10 13 14 03 04 07 02 03 04 14 09 06
01 02 03 01 02 14 15 04 05 15 05 10 11 12 13 14 01 02

Exercises

1. REARRANGE

Exercise. Changing the arrangement of the pieces is what playing with the Ball of Whacks is all about. Take a piece from one part of the Ball and move it somewhere else. Do this a dozen times. You've got a different shape. Now, create a pleasing design. Admire it for a few moments. When you're finished, rearrange the pieces into something completely different.

Background. Rearranging is one of nature's prime methods of creation. The moving plates of the earth's crust form new land masses and surface features. The shuffling of the DNA genetic deck through sex produces new life forms.

In human affairs, rearrangement plays an equally significant role. In sports, a coach might juggle his lineup to improve team performance. In business, a manager might reorganize personnel to take advantage of changing market conditions. In warfare, a military commander might deploy troops in an unorthodox manner to outmaneuver an enemy.

In film, a screenwriter might alter the typical story-line to create a more compelling thriller. In music, a composer might reorchestrate a score's instrumentation to alter its feeling. And, in decorating, a designer might reorder the contents of a room to give it more warmth.

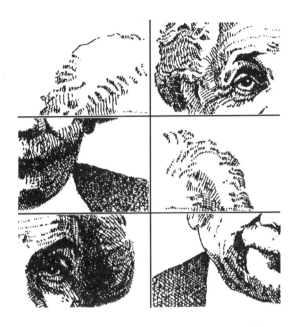

Questions. Imagine that you can rearrange things in your problem as easily as you rearrange the different pieces of the Ball of Whacks. Where would you start? Try putting your ending in the middle. Or the center on the top. Or the inside on the outside. Or the left on the right. How can you reposition the components of your problem? Where can you be more flexible?

2. COMBINE

Exercise. Combine the pieces with some outside materials — perhaps some metal ones such as ball bearings, paper clips, or a cookie baking sheet — and incorporate them into a design. What's now possible? Are there new play opportunities? What other materials can you bring in? How about a deck of cards? How about a collaborative design with a complete stranger?

Background. Combining unusual ideas is at the heart of the creative process. Inventors combine components to craft new products: Gutenberg joined together the wine press and the coin punch to create moveable type and the printing press. Entrepreneurs bring together resources from different arenas to build new businesses: Joseph Pulitzer added large-scale advertising to high speed printing to create the mass-circulation newspaper.

Engineers mix different materials to create new ones: ancient Greek metallurgists alloyed soft copper with even softer tin to product hard bronze. And, scientists marry diverse concepts to produce new models of explanation: naturalist Charles Darwin combined the idea of random genetic mutations with natural selection to arrive at his theory of evolution.

Questions. What unusual ideas can you combine with your issue? Pick two of the following professions: chef, soldier, software developer, talk show host, cheerleader, minister, politican, quarterback, gardener, trial lawyer, test pilot, and florist. Suppose a member from the two professions you selected collaborated to give you suggestions on your problem. What advice would they give you?

3. SUBSTITUTE

Exercise. Remove four or more pieces from the Ball. Now go find or make some shapes that you can fit into the gaps. Perhaps a piece of aluminum foil that's been balled up. Or maybe some clay. Or make some new pieces out of card board. How can you substitute the individual pieces for other things? Can you drill holes in them and use them as components in a mobile? Or perhaps in a necklace? Use them as money?

Background. "Accept no substitutes" could never be the motto of the creative process. Indeed, much of human progress is the result of substituting one idea, thing, or process for another: words for grunts, tools for fingers, money for goods. If you've ever used a potato for a radio antenna, or created a knife from a broken light bulb, you have this ability.

Much of creativity is the ability to take something out of one context and put it into another so that it takes on new meanings. The first person to look at an oyster and think "food" had this ability. So did the first person to look at sheep intestines and think "guitar strings," and the first person to look at a perfume vaporizer and think "gasoline carburetor," and the first person to look at bacterial mold and think "antibiotics."

Questions. Nothing is irreplaceable. Just as you substituted for the pieces in the Ball of Whacks, what can you substitute for in the various pieces of your situation? What's the most expensive component? What's the most time-consuming? The most boring? What are the most enjoyable parts? What can you substitute for them? What words do you use when you define your problem? What different words can you use? What different places do they lead your thinking?

4. DROP AN ASSUMPTION

Exercise. What assumptions can you drop about how you play with the Ball of Whacks? That you can't break open a piece and change its magnets? That you can't play with it in the dark or underwater? That you can't put the pieces on a cake or in soup? That you can't write on the pieces or paint them? That you can't break up the set by giving away individual pieces?

Background. Folklore has it that the explorer Columbus challenged some Spanish courtiers to stand an egg on its end. They tried but weren't able to keep it from rolling over. Columbus then hard-boiled one and and squashed one end of it to create a base. "That's not fair," they protested. "Don't be silly," he replied, "you just assumed way more than necessary."

Our assumptions are great for most of what we do, but at times they can limit our thinking. The inventor Thomas Edison had a simple test he used to measure the mental openness of prospective employees. He'd invite a candidate to lunch and serve a bowl of soup. He'd then watch to see whether the person salted his soup before tasting it. If he did, he wouldn't be offered the job. Edison felt that people are more open to different possibilities if they don't salt their experience of life before tasting it.

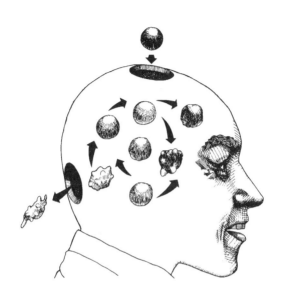

Questions. What unnecessary assumptions can you drop in your issue? In what ways are you "salting your experience" before tasting it? What "time" and "scheduling" assumptions can you let go of? How about "people" and "place" assumptions? What assumptions would a kindergarten teacher challenge in your problem? A jazz drummer? A professional wrestler? A mime? A mystic? A graphic designer? A bomb de-fuser? A policeman? A trial attorney? A standup comedian?

5. FIND A PATTERN

Exercise. What patterns do you recognize? What different ways do the pieces converge? Which ways do the magnets attract and repel? How many rhombus patterns can you make? What patterns do you notice in how you play with it? Are there certain times of the day you're more playful? Are you more playful by yourself or with others?

Background. Much of what we call "intelligence" is our ability to recognize patterns. For example, imagine that you're watching television with some friends. Someone walks into the room, trips over a chair and knocks it down. What's your impression of this person? That he's a klutz, right? Five minutes later, another person walks in, and she too knocks over the chair. Ten minutes later, the whole scene is repeated. What's your opinion now? Probably that the chair is in the wrong place and should be moved. Nice going, you've recognized a pattern!

We find patterns everywhere, from noticing that terminally ill nursing-home patients are more likely to die after a holiday than before it, to seeing that an arc through the square portions of nestling *golden rectangles* will describe a *golden spiral*. Remember the adage: "Once is an instance, twice may be a coincidence, but three or more times make a pattern."

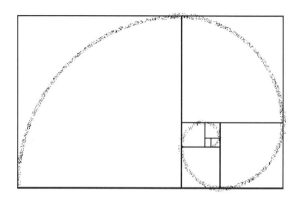

Questions. What patterns do you see in your situation? What is the relationship of the various components to the whole? Which parts dominate? Which are subservient? Do certain parts attract or repel other parts? What tends to stay in the background? Are there certain rhythms in which things seem to take place? What "unexpected" patterns do you see? How can you use them to better understand your issue?

6. SIMPLIFY

Exercise. What is the simplest shape you can create with Ball of Whacks? (No, this isn't a trick question.) It is a fully assembled Ball? Is it single piece? Is it all the pieces spread out? Is it a star? Is it two pieces showing the attractive forces in operation? Is it a diagram of the shape? Perhaps the simplest shape is just the *thought* of making a shape. Or maybe it's not doing anything at all.

Background. Editor: "I like your book except for the ending." Author: "What's wrong with the ending?" Editor: "It should be much closer to the beginning."

Questions. How can you simplify your situation? What is the simplest form you can create? What can you edit out of it to make it better? What can you streamline? Where would "less" be "more"? What if you didn't do anything?

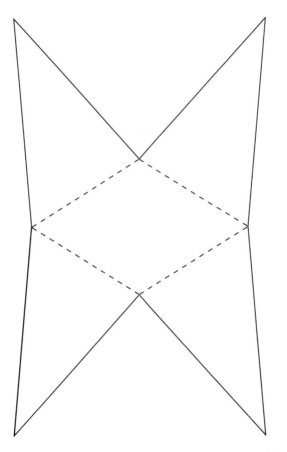

7. SEE THE OBVIOUS

Exercise. Take a moment and write down the ten most obvious things you can think of about the Ball of Whacks. For example, you might say that the faces are rhombi. The magnetic pieces attract one another. It's a prop for a series of creativity exercises. It has a homonymic name (sounds like "ball of wax"). It has pyramids. What else?

Background. Sometimes the most helpful ideas are right in front of us, but we fail to see them. For example, if you study the evolution of the bicycle during the 1860s and 1870s, you'll notice that both wheels started out at about the same size. Over time, however, the front wheel got larger, and the rear wheel became smaller. The reason was that the pedals were attached directly to the front wheel. Since there was no drive-train on the bicycle, the only way to make the bike go faster was to make the front wheel bigger. The culmination of this trend was the "penny farthing" model with a front wheel almost 1.5 meters in diameter. Needless to say, such bicycles weren't very safe. The curious thing is that the solution for a better and safer bicycle was right in front of the bicycle designers. The bicycles themselves were manufactured using drive-train technology! Finally, someone made the obvious connection, and asked, "Why not use a drive-train to power the rear wheel?" Within a few years this safer model completely replaced the penny farthing.

Questions. "Only the most foolish of mice would hide in a cat's ear," says designer Scott Love, "but only the wisest of cats would think to look there." What are you overlooking in your current situation? What resources and solutions are right in front of you? If you step back away from your situation, what are the five most obvious things you can say about it? What are two obvious contexts in which you haven't thought about your problem?

8. LAUGH AT IT

Exercise. What's funny about the Ball of Whacks? Make up a few funny names for it, for example: "Hairball of Whacks," or "Air Ball of Whacks." Think of a silly game you can play with it. What oddball shapes you can make?

Background. Where do you find a dog with no legs? Where you left him! How do you kill a circus? Go for the juggler! What's the difference between a magician and a behavioral psychologist? The psychologist pulls habits out of rats!

Humor is a lot of fun. But that's not all! There's a close relationship between the "ha-ha" of humor and the "Aha!" of discovery. For example, one day a new product design team got into a really crazy mood and made fun of their product. The meeting was a great success, and many ideas were generated. The next week, everybody was in a serious mood and no new ideas were generated.

If you can laugh at a problem, perhaps you'll overturn a few assumptions and come up with some fresh ideas. Indeed, the mental strategies underlying humor — for example, combining different ideas, asking unusual "what if" questions, parodying the rules — are congruent with effective problem-solving techniques. As physicist Niels Bohr once put it, "There are some things that are so serious that you have to laugh at them."

Questions. Remember: it's not so important to be serious as it is to be serious about the important things. The monkey has an expression of seriousness that would do credit to any great scholar. But the monkey is serious because he itches. What can you take less seriously? What's funny about your issue? What crazy, zany things can you do to it? What can you laugh at in your situation that you usually find objectionable?

9. REVERSE

Exercise. Reverse the way you usually play with the Ball of Whacks. If you usually try to make something beautiful, make something ugly. If you usually play with it by yourself, then do it with others. If you're a male, imagine that you're a female and play with it from that perspective, and vice versa.

Background. Reversing how you look at a situation helps you see it in a new way. For example, in the late 1950s, many drivers in Seattle began finding small pockmarks on their windshields. Some people believed that atomic tests by the Russians had contaminated the atmosphere and this was returning to earth in a glass-etching dew. Another theory suggested that tiny acid drops from Seattle's recently constructed roads were being flung against the windshields. Some experts investigated the mystery and found that the pitting was an old phenomenon, not a new one. All windshields develop "scars" as a car ages; it's part of normal wear. The mass hysteria developed because as the reports of pitting came to the attention of more people, they checked their own cars, usually by looking through the glass from the *outside* of the car. What had broken out was an epidemic not of windshield pitting, but of *reverse* windshield viewing. By reversing their viewpoint, people discovered something that had always been there but they had never noticed.

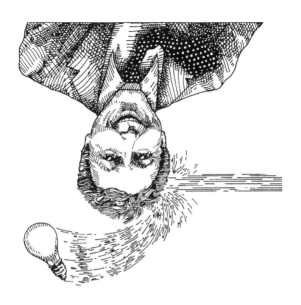

Questions. How can you reverse your viewpoint? What's the "most important" part of your issue or problem? What if you viewed it as inconsequential? What's the unfriendliest part? What if you viewed it as your "best buddy?" What's the "most serious" part? What if you viewed it as the "most playful?" What is the "most time-consuming" part? What if you just ignored it?

10. MAKE USE OF THE RANDOM

Exercise. Let the whack pieces come together in random ways. Try placing a dozen or so pieces on a flat surface so that they're not touching. Now slowly push them together, and let the pieces assemble themselves in a random way. Look at the resulting arrangements for a little bit. What patterns and pictures emerge? What new possible shapes do you see? How can you build on them? Try adding other materials and repeat the exercise. What ideas does this stimulate?

Background. There once was an Indian medicine man who made hunting maps for his tribe. Whenever game got sparse, he'd put a piece of fresh leather in the sun to dry. Then he'd fold and twist it in is hands, say a few prayers over it, and then smooth it out. The rawhide was now etched with lines. He then marked some reference points on the rawhide, and — presto! — a new game map was created. When the hunters followed the map's newly defined trails, they usually discovered abundant game. By letting the rawhide's random folds represent trails, he pointed the hunters to places they had not looked.

Since we tend to use the same-problem solving approaches repeatedly, we usually come up with the same answers. Random information can force us to look at our problems in new ways, and this can do wonders to stir our thinking.

Questions. Open your mind up to things that have nothing in common with your current situation. Pick out the 13th word of page 311 of your dictionary. How does it relate to what you're doing. Look out your window and find the first thing that has blue in it. How would it help solve your problem? Open the obituary section from your newspaper and read the first two "obits." What can you apply to your situation from these people's lives? What random ideas can you connect to a current problem?

11. IMAGINE HOW OTHERS WOULD DO IT

Exercise. For a few moments, imagine that you are the classical music composer Mozart. Now create some designs that are pleasing to you, and that reflect your genius. Now imagine that you are Homer Simpson. What designs can you make?

Background. A good way to stretch your imagination is to ask "what if" someone else were solving your problem. How would this person — for example, Winston Churchill, the Godfather, your mother, the Three Stooges, Mother Tersesa, the Buddha, Beethoven, or a seven year old girl — go about it? What assumptions would they bring in? What constraints would they ignore? What special twists would they give to it? What special expertise would they add?

For example, let's suppose that you're the principal of a high school. You wonder: what if someone with a mindset like Walt Disney had your job? What things would change? There might be more emphasis on graphics and visual learning. Students would learn through experience. Imagine the playground: students would learn physics and engineering from building rides for the school. The motto would be: "If you don't take risks, you won't achieve your dreams." Students would enjoy school thus boosting attendance.

Questions. Whom do you respect for creative achievement? A leader in your field? A teacher? A parent? Now imagine one of them is responsible for developing your concept. What would they do? How would they approach it? Who's been in the news lately? How would they solve your problem? Who is your favorite artist or musician? How would this person go about it?

12. IMAGINE YOU'RE THE IDEA

Exercise. Imagine you're the Ball of Whacks. How does it feel when different pieces are pulled apart or stuck together? Do you enjoy the "click" you make? Do you like it when your pieces are arranged in different designs? Where do you like to be played with? Create a shape or mosaic that reflects how you are feeling.

Background. Identifying with your issue is a great way to get a different perspective. For example, suppose you're trying to improve the design of a toaster. What would it be like to actually be a toaster? How would you receive bread? What's it like when your heating elements go on? What happens when seeds fall to the bottom?

Imagine that you're a parking meter. How does it feel when coins are inserted in you? What's it like when you're "expired." What sounds might you make? How could you be easier to use?

The results of playful speculation can yield quite practical results. A noted scientist once asked himself, "What if I were an elevator falling through space at the speed of light, and a shaft of light entered the elevator? What would the light's behavior be?" By investigating such possibilities, Albert Einstein developed some of his early relativity concepts.

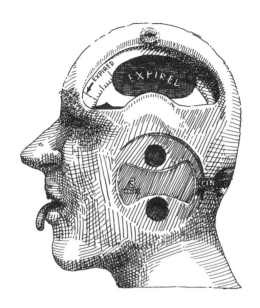

Questions. How would you feel if you were the idea you're developing? If your problem were a person, what kind of attributes would it have? How old would it be? Sociable or reclusive? Athletic? Intellectual? Would it have brothers and sisters? Who are its parents? Does it have children? What kinds of pets does it have? What are its politics? Does it have any hobbies? What about its religion? What does it believe in?

13. COMPARE

Exercise. What is playing with the Ball of Whacks similar to? What activities can you compare it with? Planting a garden? Doing a crossword puzzle? Finger painting? Sculpting? Having a discussion with a teenager? Prospecting for gold?

Background. Philosopher Ortega y Gassett: "The metaphor is probably the most fertile power possessed by man." The key to metaphorical thinking is comparing unrelated things and finding similarities between them. Example: what do a cat and a refrigerator have in common? They both have a place to put fish; they both have tails; they purr; they come in a variety of colors; and, they both last about fifteen years.

Finding similarity is how our thinking grows: we understand the unfamiliar by comparing it to what we know. The first automobiles were called "horseless carriages." Early locomotives were dubbed "iron horses." Many great teachers have used metaphors to express their ideas. Socrates compared the human mind to a "ship in which the sailors had mutinied and locked up the Captain below." Jesus likened the Kingdom of God to a "wedding feast." And, Chinese philosopher Lao-tzu employed the concept of the "empty of hub of a thirty-spoked wheel" to describe the ineffable nature of the *Tao*.

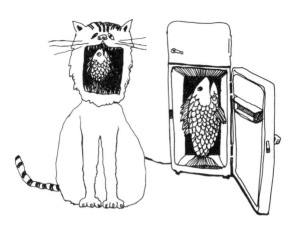

Questions. What metaphors can you make for your issue? What similarities does your idea have with cooking a meal? Building a house? Raising a child? Selling a product? Running a marathon? Starting a revolution? Courting a mate? Putting out a fire? Fighting a disease? Having a baby? How is your issue similar to selling a product? Suing an adversary? Running a marathon? Doing standup comedy? Colonizing a territory? Going fishing? Arranging flowers? Pruning a tree? Conducting an orchestra? What can you learn from these activities that would shed light on your own situation?

14. LOOK TO NATURE

Exercise. What in nature looks like the Ball of Whacks? What shapes can you create that look like natural shapes? Can you make some flower shapes? Animals? Insects? How about molecules? Rock formations? Crystals?

Background. Many good ideas have been discovered because someone borrowed a pattern or principle from nature and then applied it to his situation. The sticky hooked spine of the common burr inspired the man who invented Velcro fastener. The "spinning wing" feature of the elm seed served as a model for more efficient windmills and helicopters. Bell invented the telephone by imitating the ear. Nineteenth-century English gardener Joseph Paxton modeled his design of the world's first glass-and-iron building, the Crystal Palace, on his studies of the cantilevered rib structure of the giant water lily *Victoria amazonica*.

Biologist Julian Vincent developed a smart clothing fabric that adjusts to changing body temperatures by studying how pine cones open and close depending on the humidity. And, database developer Eric Lumer created a more flexible customer-profiling system for the banking industry by studying how worker ants cluster their dead when cleaning their nests.

Questions. What patterns and cycles in nature can you use to develop your idea? What can you borrow from the following? The seasons of the year. The creation of compost. Natural selection. Creating hybrid plants. The life cycle of a mountain range. Earthquakes. How beavers build dams. Think of a letter of the alphabet. Now think of an animal (mammal, fish, bird, insect, etc.) that begins with that letter. What two specific tactics would that animal try in dealing with your problem?

15. ASK A FOOL

Exercise. What are some really foolish things you can do with the Ball of Whacks? What odd places can you use it? While giving testimony at a court trial? During a job interview? What weird and foolish shapes can you make?

Background. Listening to a fool is what Renaissance kings did to break out of the group-think environment their "yes-men" advisors created. It was the fool's job to parody any proposal under discussion to make it appear in a fresh light. He might extol the trivial, trifle the exalted, or reverse the common perception of a situation. Example: "If a man is sitting backwards on a horse, why do we assume that it is the man who is backwards and not the horse?" Result: he dislodged people's assumptions and helped them see things in a new way.

An example of how the fool opens our thinking is Till Eulenspiegel, the 14th-century German peasant trickster whose merry pranks were the source of numerous folk tales. One day when Till was hiking in the mountains, he was seen to be crying while walking downhill and laughing merrily while climbing up. When asked the reason for his odd behavior, Till replied, "While going downhill I'm thinking of the strenuous climb up ahead and that makes me sad; and, while hiking uphill I'm anticipating the pleasure of the easy descent."

Questions. As educator Rudolph Flesch put it, "Creative thinking may simply mean the realization that there's no particular virture in doing things the way they've always been done." What conventional wisdom can you challenge? Suppose a fool told you that you are absolutely wrong in your two most basic assumptions about your issue. Think of some reasons why he is correct.

Summary

The Ball of Whacks is a lot of fun to play with. But that's not all! It's also a wonderful vehicle for use in a creativity workshop. Just combine it with a problem or issue, and apply the creativity exercises, strategies, and questions in this section. Whether you employ "Drop An Assumption," "Look to Nature," "See the Obvious," or any of the other strategies, your thinking will be headed in fresh directions. The result: more than likely you'll come up with some new insights into your situation.

Even if you don't have a particular issue you want to make the focus of a workshop, using the Ball with the creativity exercises is a great way to get your thinking warmed up. Consider this: if you spend some time consciously rearranging, reversing, comparing, and substituting the various Whack pieces, how difficult can it be for you subsequently to do the very same thing with the different elements of your problem?

Part 3:

The Inspiration for the Ball of Whacks and Other Golden Information

The Idea

I love playing with polyhedra. I've been making these geometric solids since I was a kid, and I swear by them to stimulate my creative juices. Indeed, when I started my company (Creative Think) some years back, I spent a lot of time constructing dodecahedrons (12-sided solids) and icosahedrons (20-sided).

A few years ago, I was looking for a 30-sided polyhedron for a project I was working on: I wanted an object on which I could display thirty different sayings from the ancient Greek philosopher Heraclitus. These included: "You can't step in the same river twice," "Dogs bark at what they don't understand," "Your character is your destiny," and, "Expect the unexpected or you won't find it."

During my search, I discovered a shape that consists of thirty identical rhombi. (If you remember your high school geometry, a rhombus is a four-sided equilateral with two pairs of parallel sides.) It is called the *rhombic triacontahedron* (from the Greek *triaconta* for "thirty" and *hedron* for "side"). Because its name can be a real mouthful, I shall henceforth refer to the rhombic triacontahedron as the "RT."

I made several models of the RT, and I found it to be not only a great manipulation object, but also a truly beautiful shape.

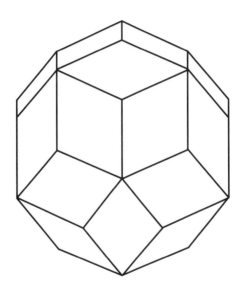

Rhombic Triacontahedron

One feature I particularly liked about the RT is its relationship to two of my favorite polyhedra, the dodecahedron and icosahedron. Indeed, it seems as though the RT has both a dodecahedron and an icosahedron "living" within it. If you connect the short diagonals of each of the rhombic faces, you will get the edges of a dodecahedron. And, if you connect the long diagonals, you'll get the edges of an icosahedron. I thought this was pretty cool!

Partial Outline of a Dodecahedron around a Triacontahedron

Partial Outline of an Icosahedron around a Triacontahedron

So, I befriended a very special polyhedron, and, of course, I spent a lot of time playing it. But the more I tossed and flipped it, the more I thought, "How can I improve its playability?"

As I thought about these questions, I realized that I had been focusing on the ball's surface. I decided to change my viewpoint, and I imagined looking at the RT's center. And then I had a key insight: "What if I were able to break this ball into thirty identical pieces? Why not create thirty pyramids with each rhombus face forming a pyramid base and the RT's center forming the pyramid's apex?"

Rhombic Pyramid Section in a RT

I made some models and the idea worked! All thirty pyramids fit compactly together. But when these pieces were apart they could be played with and turned into other designs. I was thrilled!

Then I had another thought, "What if I could get these pieces to stick together?" Almost immediately, I had the idea of putting a magnet into each face of every piece. That worked as well!

Bingo! I had created a special set of building blocks with the following qualities:

▲ Both the whole shape and the individual pieces are **beautiful**;

▲ The pieces are a lot of **fun** to play with;

▲ The ball is **easy** to reassemble back into the original ball shape (it's not really a puzzle, but if it were, its puzzle-rating would be "very simple"); and,

▲ It gets me into a **creative** frame of mind.

The Ball of Whacks™ was born!

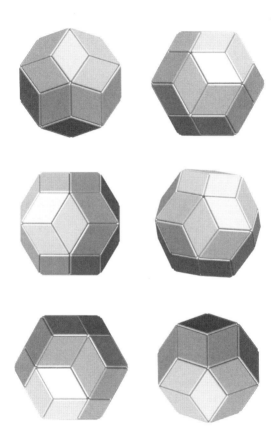

The Golden Ratio

Here is a good place to mention an important characteristic of each Whack piece, namely its "golden" nature. Let me explain. The rhombus base has a pair of 63.43° angles and a pair of 116.57° angles. If you measure the long diagonal and short diagonal, and compare them, you'll discover that they have a ratio of 1.618. Recognize that number? It's ϕ (phi), also known as the *golden ratio*.

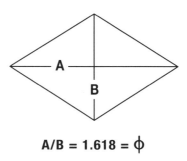

A/B = 1.618 = ϕ

Thus, each Whack piece's base is a *golden rhombus* because it conforms to the *golden ratio!* Indeed, a *golden rhombus* can be inscribed in a *golden rectangle* (the rhombus's vertices are the rectangle's midpoints).

Here's some background. The *golden ratio* is derived by dividing a line in such a way that the ratio of the longer segment (AB) to the shorter segment (BC) is the same as the ratio of the length of the entire line (AC) to the longer segment (AB).★

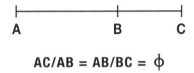

$$AC/AB = AB/BC = \phi$$

Supposedly, Pythagoras discovered the *golden ratio*. The ancient Greeks incorporated it into their art and architecture. An example is the Parthenon in Athens. Its design employed the *golden rectangle* — thought to be the most beautiful of all rectangles.

★ The numerical value of the *golden ratio* is $1/2 + (\sqrt{5})/2$ or approximately 1.618033988. The symbol used for the *golden ratio* is ϕ (phi). Interestingly enough, its reciprocal $(1/\phi)$ is equal to 0.618033988, or ϕ - 1. Even more fascinating, the square of the *golden ratio* (ϕ^2) equals 2.618033988 or ϕ + 1. The German mathematician Johannes Kepler had high praise for the golden ratio: "Geometry has two great treasures: one the Theorem of Pythagoras; the other, the division of a line into extreme and mean ratio [the *golden ratio*]. The first we may compare to a measure of gold; the second we may name a precious jewel."

Create your own *golden rectangle* (6). Start with a square (1). Next, draw a straight line from the midpoint of the baseline to the square's upper-right hand corner (2). Use that line as a radius and draw an arc down to the baseline (3). Extend the baseline out to where it intersects the arc (4). Finally, add two lines to fill out the reactangle (5). The ratio of the rectangle's two sides is 1.618 to 1 or ϕ.

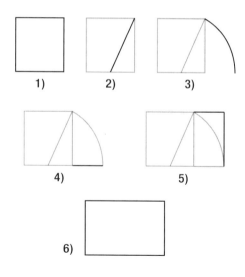

1) 2) 3)

4) 5)

6)

The *golden ratio* pops up in some surprising areas of mathematics. For example, the ratio of consecutive Fibonacci numbers (1, 1, 2, 3, 5, 8, 13, 21, 34, 55, 89, 144 . . . where each number is the sum of the previous two numbers) approaches the *golden ratio* of ϕ as the sequence gets higher. These numbers describe such things as the number of members in successive generations of rabbits, the growing points in branching plants, the arrangement of seeds in a sunflower, and the coil of a ocean wave.

The *golden ratio* is also found in art. Some of the paintings of Sandro Botticelli, Leonardo da Vinci, Franz Hals, J.M.W. Turner, Marcel Duchamp, and Georges Braque, among others, are laid out in accordance with the guidelines of ϕ. The architect Le Corbusier strongly advocated its application to art and architecture; and, Frank Lloyd Wright based his spiral-ramped design of the Guggenheim Museum in New York on the *golden ratio* spiral structure of the chambered nautilus.

This is probably more than enough *golden ratio* information, but I hope it helps you appreciate the "goldenness" in the Ball of Whacks' geometric DNA.

The Geometry of the Whack Piece

Each Whack piece in the Ball of Whacks is a right *golden* rhombic pyramid. The term "right" refers to the fact that the pyramid's apex is perpendicular to its base's centroid (the intersection point of the base's two diagonals). The pyramid's base is a *golden* rhombus. That means the ratio of its long diagonal to its short diagonal is ϕ (phi), also known as the *golden ratio*, or about 1.618.

What gives this particular right *golden* rhombic pyramid its special character is its height. From centroid to apex, its height is $(\phi + 1)/2$ times the length of the short diagonal.

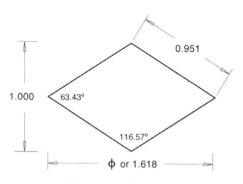

Rhombus Base View

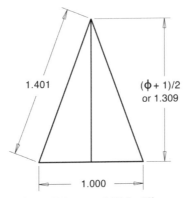

Short Diagonal Side View

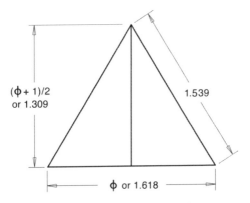

Long Diagonal Side View

Let's Give the Hand a Big Hand!

A considerable portion of the brain is dedicated to hand-related functions. Indeed, it could be argued that it was the hand's development that led to our species' increased brain size. From approximately 4,000,000 years ago to about 100,000 years ago, the hand underwent a series of significant changes that gave it more power and versatility. These changes included: 1) the thumb became longer in relation to the other four fingers; 2) the thumb became capable of touching the fourth and fifth fingers; 3) a more flexible joint developed at the base of the little finger; and, 4) the wrist developed the ability to bend forward away from the thumb.

The result was that as the hand discovered and mastered a variety of different types of grips, there became more and different ways the hand could manipulate objects and use them as tools. As the hand gained these new powers, the human brain, in turn, developed new ways of making sense of what the hand was doing. During this period, the brain grew in size (from 400 cc to its present 1350 cc) and processing power. In other words, as the hand became "handier," the brain became "brainier."

Because of this significant overlap between the sensori-motor and cognitive functions, working with our hands stimulates the brain. As novelist Robertson Davies put it, "The hand speaks to the brain as surely as the brain speaks to the hand." And this is true whether we're carving wood, peeling fruit, grasping a hammer, sewing pieces of cloth together, playing the piano, performing surgery, fixing a carburetor, shuffling cards, throwing a baseball, making gestures, massaging a muscle, or manipulating the pieces of the Ball of Whacks.

"What's A Whack?"

A "whack" is a creativity term for "something that stimulates you to think differently." I started using this term in my first book, **A Whack on the Side of the Head.** It has its origin in the following two stories.

A creativity teacher invited one of his students over to his house for afternoon tea. They talked for a bit, and then came time for tea. The teacher poured some into the student's cup. Even after the cup was full, he continued to pour. The cup overflowed and tea spilled out on to the floor.

Finally, the student said: "Master, you must stop pouring; the tea is overflowing — it's not going into the cup."

The teacher replied, "That's very observant. The same is true with you. If you are to receive any of my teachings, you must first empty out your mental cup."

Moral: We need the ability to unlearn what we know.

Without the ability to temporarily forget what we know, our minds remain cluttered up with

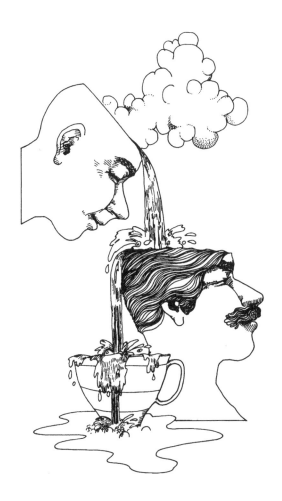

ready-made answers. One key to opening our minds is to "unlearn" what we know — to empty our mental cup. This sounds like a simple technique, but sometimes it's difficult to apply. Often we've integrated our assumptions so well into our thinking that we're no longer aware that we're being guided by them. Let's return to our creativity teacher.

At another lesson the teacher and the student are discussing a problem. Despite lengthy conversation, the student doesn't quite get the point the teacher is making.

Finally, the teacher picks up a stick and gives him a whack on the side of the head with it. Suddenly, the student begins to grasp the situation and "think something different."

Moral: Sometimes nothing short of "a whack on the side of the head" can dislodge the assumptions that keep us thinking "more of the same."

Like the student, we all need an occasional "whack on the side of the head" to shake us out of our routine assumptions, and to stimulate us to think about things in a fresh way.

"Whacks" come in all sizes, shapes, and flavors. Sometimes you'll get whacked by a problem or failure. Sometimes it'll be the result of a joke or a paradox. And sometimes it will be a surprise or unexpected situation. These whacks all have one thing in common: they force you to change your assumptions and "think something different."

There are times when a whack on the side of the head can be the best thing to happen to you. It might help you spot a potential problem before it arises. It could help you discover an opportunity that wasn't previously apparent. Or it could help you generate some new ideas. At the very least, it stimulates you to think.

And this is where the Ball of Whacks comes in. You look at this aesthetically pleasing ball, and think, "That's nice. I wonder what it does?" And then when you start playing with it, you're amazed that you can do so much. In the process, it also gets your creative juices flowing. For this reason, it has earned the right to be called the "Ball of Whacks."

About the Author

Roger von Oech's seminars, books, and products have enriched the creativity of many millions around the world. He earned his Ph.D. from Stanford University in the "History of Ideas." He enjoys masters swimming, travel, and reading history and science. He lives with his wife in northern California.

Sunrise at Angkor Wat, Cambodia.
The author, with a young Buddhist monk
who is turning the Ball of Whacks into a sun.

From the Author

I hope you enjoy playing with your Ball of Whacks. This tool has been a joy to create and develop.

I'd love to hear your ideas about and uses for the Ball of Whacks. You can reach me at:

roger@creativethink.com

or at my website:

www.creativethink.com

You can also reach me at my mailing address:

Roger von Oech
Creative Think
Box 7354
Menlo Park, California
USA 94026